Why Do My Teeth Fall Out?

By Isabella Willebrandt

Gareth Stevens
Publishing

Please visit our website, www.garethstevens.com. For a free color catalog of all our high-quality books, call toll free 1-800-542-2595 or fax 1-877-542-2596.

Library of Congress Cataloging-in-Publication Data

Willebrandt, Isabella.
Why do my teeth fall out? / by Isabella Willebrandt.
    p. cm. — (My body does strange stuff!)
Includes index.
ISBN 978-1-4824-0299-5 (pbk.)
ISBN 978-1-4824-0300-8 (6-pack)
ISBN 978-1-4824-0296-4 (library binding)
1. Teeth — Juvenile literature. 2. Deciduous teeth — Juvenile literature. I. Title.
QP88.6 W55 2014
611—dc23

Published in 2014 by
Gareth Stevens Publishing
111 East 14th Street, Suite 349
New York, NY 10003

Designer: Michael J. Flynn
Editor: Greg Roza

Photo credits: Cover, pp. 1, 15 Zurijeta/Shutterstock.com; p. 5 Paul Simcock/ Photodisc/Getty Images; p. 7 (mouth with teeth) Vectomart/Shutterstock.com; pp. 7 (teeth insets), 9 GRei/Shutterstock.com; p. 11 Gelpi JM/Shutterstock.com; p. 13 Hannamariah/Shutterstock.com; p. 17 Andre Blais/Shutterstock.com; p. 19 Jeff Vinnick/Getty Images; p. 21 Jacek Chabraszewski/Shutterstock.com.

Printed in the United States of America

CPSIA compliance information: Batch #CW14GS: For further information contact Gareth Stevens, New York, New York at 1-800-542-2595.

Contents

Boldface words appear in the glossary.

My Tooth Fell Out!

As you grow older, your body goes through many changes. Your teeth are no different. Your baby teeth grow in when you are very little. As you get older, the baby teeth fall out. Ever wonder why? Let's find out!

5

Chompers!

Our front teeth are called incisors (ihn-SY-zuhrz). We use them to cut our food into smaller pieces. Next to the incisors are the canines. They're pointy and help cut food, too. In the back of our mouth, the molars **grind** food.

KNOW YOUR TEETH

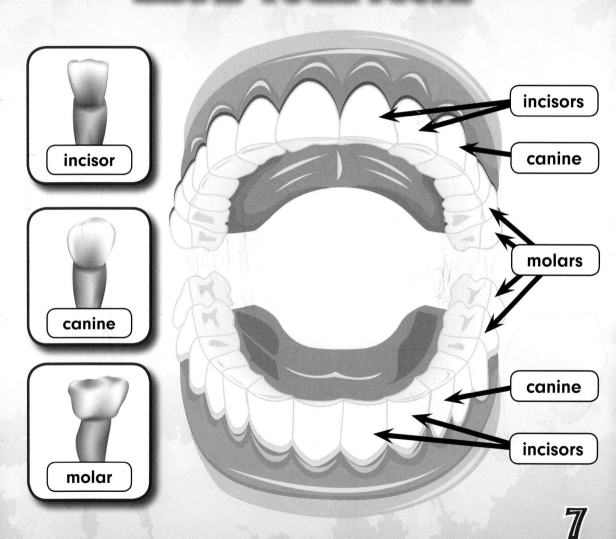

incisor

canine

molar

incisors

canine

molars

canine

incisors

7

Outside and Inside

The part of a tooth you can see is the crown. It's covered with a very hard **tissue** called enamel. Enamel keeps our teeth healthy. The part of a tooth stuck in your gum and jaw is the root. The root isn't covered with enamel.

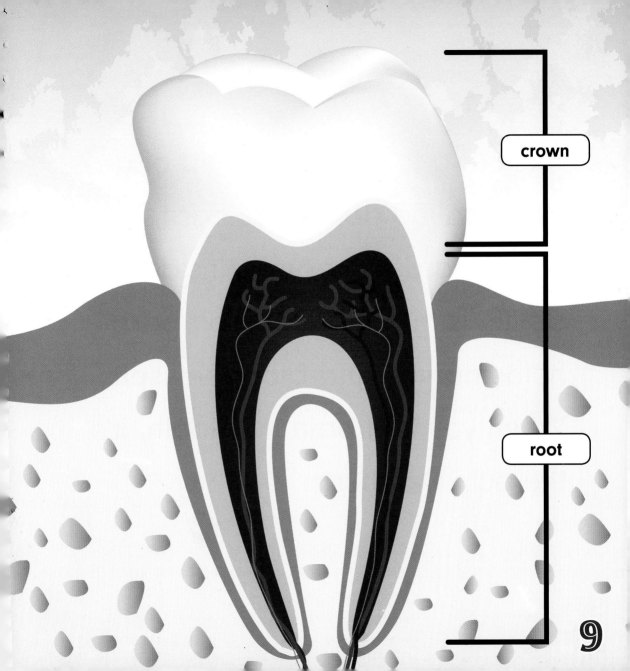

crown

root

9

Most of a tooth is made up of a tissue called dentin. It's hard, but not as hard as enamel. Inside the dentin is the pulp. This soft part holds **nerves** and **blood vessels**. When you feel pain in a tooth, it's the pulp that hurts.

11

Baby Teeth

Our baby teeth come in when we're between 6 months and 2 1/2 years old. These teeth are also called **primary** teeth. Most kids have 20 baby teeth. They're smaller than adult teeth. They also wear down faster than adult teeth.

13

In time, a baby tooth becomes loose. This is because the tooth's root breaks down. The root is what held the tooth in place. Now, you can wiggle the tooth. In time, the tooth will be so loose it will just fall out!

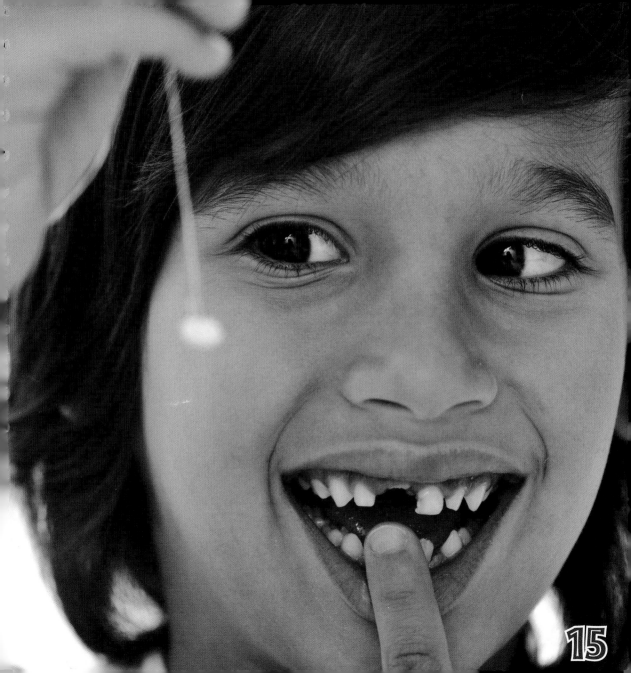

Adult Teeth

Baby teeth often start to fall out around age 5 or 6. They do this because our adult teeth, or **permanent** teeth, push them out of the way. This may continue until you're about 13 years old. Most adults have 32 permanent teeth.

17

Fake Teeth?

Adult teeth are called permanent because they're supposed to last the rest of our lives. However, teeth sometimes get knocked out! A dentist can sometimes put a lost tooth back in. Or, the lost tooth can be replaced with a fake tooth.

19

Brush, Brush, Brush!

Enamel is the hardest tissue in the human body! However, it can break down over time. Some foods and drinks, such as those that contain sugar, cause teeth to **decay**. You can avoid tooth decay by brushing your teeth after every meal.

Glossary

blood vessel: a small tube in a person's body that carries blood

decay: rot

grind: to crush something into smaller pieces

nerve: a part of the body that sends messages to the brain and allows us to feel things

permanent: lasting a long time

primary: first

tissue: matter that forms the parts of living things

For More Information

Books

Kenah, Katharine. *Fascinating! Human Bodies.* Greensboro, NC: Spectrum, 2013.

Royston, Angela. *Tooth Decay.* Mankato, MN: Black Rabbit Books, 2009.

Smith, Siân. *Caring for Your Teeth.* Chicago, IL: Heinemann Library, 2013.

Websites

Healthy Teeth
www.healthyteeth.org
Learn everything you need to know about your teeth, including flouride, braces, how to avoid tooth decay, and much more.

Your Teeth
kidshealth.org/kid/htbw/teeth.html#
Read more about your teeth and how to care for them.

Index